THE
FOUR CARDINAL VIRTUES.

BY THE

REV. J. B. FIGGIS, M.A.,

AUTHOR OF

"CHRIST AND FULL SALVATION,"

"LESSONS LEARNT IN ITALY AND THE RIVIERA," &c.

*Minister of the
Countess of Huntingdon's Church, North Street, Brighton.*

London:
S. W. PARTRIDGE & CO., 9, PATERNOSTER ROW.
Brighton:
D. B. FRIEND, 77, WESTERN ROAD.

141. n. 402.

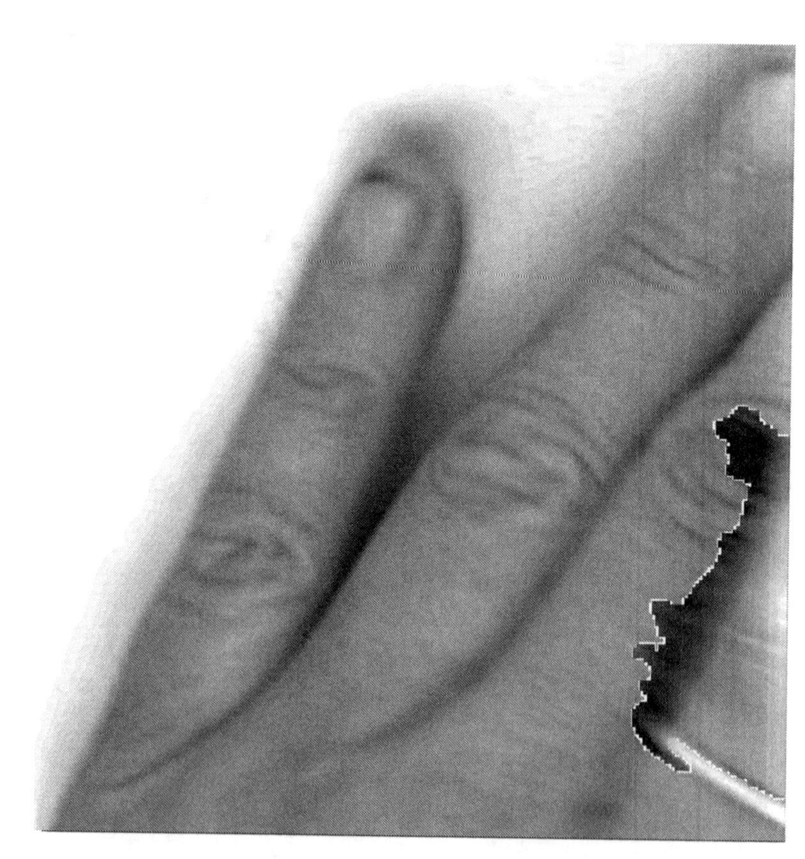

THE
FOUR CARDINAL VIRTUES

BY THE

REV. J. B. FIGGIS, M.A.

AUTHOR OF
"CHRIST AND FULL SALVATION,"
"... EARNT IN ...," ETC.

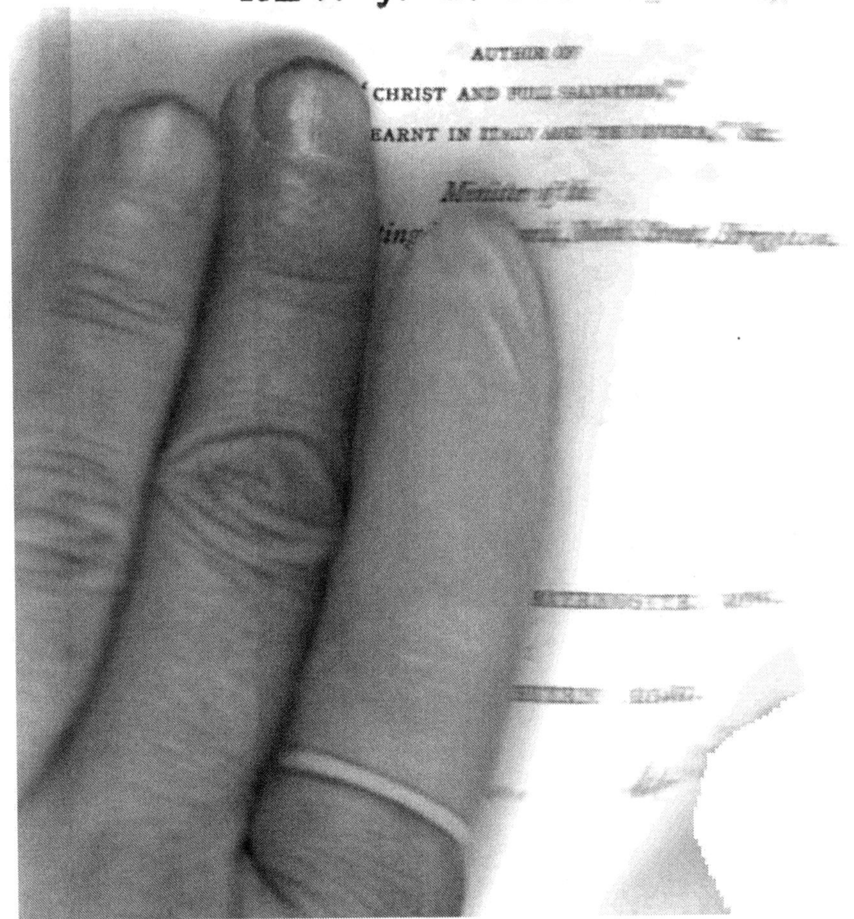

D. B. FRIEND,

PUBLISHER, PRINTER, AND BOOKSELLER,

77, WESTERN ROAD,

BRIGHTON.

To
My Sons.

"If a man love righteousness, her labours are
virtues : for she teacheth temperance and prudence,
justice and fortitude : which are such things as men
can have nothing more profitable in their life ? "—
Wisdom of Solomon, VIII. 7.

"The State, being a perfect one, must exhibit in
itself the four cardinal virtues.   Not that everyone
of its citizens must exhibit all perfectly, but the
philosophical rulers represent *prudence*, courageous
standing-army courage (*fortitude*) the well-con-
ducted populace and craftsmen *temperance*.   The
remaining virtue *justice*, the virtue of the whole,
the principle and cause of the existence of the
other three, compelling each portion of the State
to keep to its own business, and to abstain from
all interference with the affairs of the other
portions."—*Plato, Republic, Book IV.*

"Our city should be perfectly good ; it is evident
then that it is wise, brave, temperate, and just."—
Republic, IV., c. 6.

"Plato says, ' There are four virtues, prudence,
temperance, justice, fortitude, and on these are
attendant two vices, according to excess and
defect.' "—*Hippolytus, Bishop of Rome.*

PREFACE.

In a letter received a few months back from an able and earnest writer occurs this passage :—
"I am not sure whether a higher conception of Christian ethics is not necessary before the Church can grasp the truth that Christian righteousness is Christ's righteousness." I felt fortified when I received this in a conviction of my own, that true morality—a morality steeped and saturated with the love of Christ, but still, dealt with practically and in detail—needed more prominence than it sometimes receives.

We do not become Christians by our morality, we do not expect acceptance of the Father for our morality, but all the more are we bound by every motive of gratitude and of consistency to manifest to men a morality, the highest and best conceivable.

It would be a terrible day for piety if ever its votaries were even to appear negligent of morality. In every sphere of duty, on the contrary, loyalty to Christ requires that we should show that

" The Christian is the highest style of man."

J. B. FIGGIS.

26, Clifton Road, Brighton,
December 1st, 1882.

INDEX.

FORTITUDE.

" The virtue of prosperity is temperance ; the virtue of
adversity is fortitude."

LORD BACON.

CHAP. I.

FORTITUDE.

" Add to your faith virtue."—2 *Peter i.* 5.

WE are not saved by virtue ; we are saved
by Christ.   Christ and His Cross are the
only means of admission for any of us into
the Kingdom of God.   We must come to
Christ, cling to Christ, live Christ, if we
would enjoy the rest and the glory of
heaven ; no, we are not saved by virtue,
but we are not saved without it. " Without
holiness (and virtue is a part of holiness)
no man can see the Lord." " He that hath
My commandments and keepeth them, he
it is that loveth Me." We are saved to be
holy, are called to glory and virtue.

Among the virtues there is a hierarchy ; and some that are of pre-eminent importance in the character are called cardinal virtues. They are so called from a Latin word meaning a hinge, because all right action turns upon their practice. They are princes among virtues as the Roman Cardinals are princes of Rome. Plato and Aristotle, and the Author of the " Wisdom of Solomon," all name these four (though in varying order) : fortitude the virtue of the heart, prudence of the mind, temperance of the body, justice the balance of the whole.

Fortitude is the virtue " par excellence," according to Peter, for, probably that is what he means when he speaks of virtue here, manly courage or bravery. 'But where is her place in the Christian character, or what work has she to do in Christian life ? It was natural enough that heathen philosophers should praise it in days when so much fighting had to be done, for fortitude is a fighting virtue, but it seems much more suitable to a soldier than to a Christian, and others think so too. John Bunyan, for example ; for, while in both parts of his great allegory he brings in the character of Prudence, in neither, I think, does he mention fortitude.' Well now, as to that, I think he does—for what else is Mr. Great-Heart, a character that surely none could dispense with from those pages of delight ? And as to its being a fighting grace, does not David say that " life is a warfare," and Paul that Christ has chosen the Christian "to be a soldier ? " Oh ! yes, we shall all have need of fortitude for warfare, for work, and for suffering; things which come to all of us in all our lives. This is the virtue that makes martyrs and patriots to suffer for Christ and for country—missionaries and pioneers to labour for Christianity and for civilization, and above all it is the virtue which makes *men.* It is the very essence of all manliness ; (nor in saying that, do I forget you, my sisters, for) it is the essence of all womanliness, too; the ministering angel and the suffering angel, all that bears and all that beautifies life, owe very much to fortitude. Yes, we all need her, and we are always needing her, either as *energy to hold on*, for she is that, or as *resistance to hold back*, for she is that, too, or as *endurance to hold up*, for she is that also.

Life is made up largely of occasions in which one or other of these is in demand. For example : Life for all of us has its duties, and these will never be done unless we have learnt THE SECRET OF HOLDING ON. I owe a good deal to many of my schoolfellows ; to one of them I owe it that my attention was early called to this sentence of a fellow-commoner of my college— Sir Thos. Fowell Buxton (I have to quote from memory):—"The longer I live, the more I am convinced that the great difference between man and man is the possession of the quality of indomitable perseverance ; a purpose once formed, and then death or victory. Such determination will, with the blessing of God, achieve anything ; and no opportunities, no gifts, no talents can make a two-legged creature a man without it."

It was this quality that made the Drakes and the Raleighs who made England. It is this quality which largely accounts for the prosperity of England and the adversity of Ireland. It is this quality that has built up many a fortune and has helped to build up the state, and it is this same quality which has been so influential in projecting and carrying out schemes of philanthropy and Christian love. The world must not be left to go to ruin without an endeavour to save it. What part are you taking in that endeavour? "Give diligence" that you may take some part. I do not press you to have ambitions, but I do urge you to have aspirations—aspirations after a life well spent—and that it may be, you must be no dreamer or schemer, clever at mapping out countries to be won for Christ and content with having made the map. No, you must be the builder as well as the architect, and you must not be like the man who began to build and was not able to finish. Even as to the ordinary avocations of life, I would say, ask God to guide you to choose wisely, for the choice of a profession is a tremendous choice. Then, when you have followed Him in this matter, follow Him on into every detail, asking Him to do two things—to show you what to do, and to give you strength to do it. Your Guide will never leave you, but do you take care never to leave your Guide.

I was in a park the day I wrote part of this paper, and asked my way of a poor woman walking along the path. "That's the road," she said, pointing to a track among the trees and hills. I turned to make a note or two, and while I turned, I lost her, and I lost *it*, and that just at the critical point of my walk. It may be so with you, it will be so if you do not take care to seek guidance, and equal care to seek help. I do believe that there is a fund of strength at hand for us, for Christian work and for common work too, and we never use it, some of us, never. "It was supposed that to transmit the power of Niagara to New York a copper cable of enormous thickness would be needed ; but it has been shown that the whole electrical power might be transmitted by a fine copper wire, if only sufficiently insulated. So would it be with us if free from earth-contact,"* we might have and use the mighty power of the Mighty God.

I have been speaking of our working as if we were the builders ; and so in a sense we are. "Labourers together with God," says Paul; but he adds in the same chapter, "Ye are God's building," and the fear is that the materials of which this building is erected are such as to mar the very work of God Himself. No doubt, He can and does use the meanest materials for His glory ; but it is incontestable to my mind that the building would be far different, both in strength and in proportion, if the materials were better—if we, instead of being drifting sand, were hewn stones ; instead of being the willow or the alder, were the ebony or the oak ; in a word, if

* See " Prince in the Midst," p. 87.

our character contained more Fortitude. People fickle in friendship, shifty in work, vacillating in opinion,—what can be made of materials like these ? Something in God's hands, anything if they would be pliable there. But, still, this want of permanence is a flaw which must mar the best of buildings. Who wants characterless creatures, that may be crumpled up like so much brown paper, or thrown down like a pack of cards ? No ; whether it be for sacred or for secular work, we want people with some stamina in them, some of the energy which regards a difficulty as a thing to be overcome, and has no place for impossibility in its dictionary. Oh ! to see in the race rising up in England less of the flaccid self-indulgence which has been the ruin of so many, and more of the Fortitude which has been the joy and crown of the few. We want parents to inspire their children with a right self-reliance, and young people to pursue it earnestly, remembering, as Mr. Vaughan reminded the clergy of this diocese the other day, that " Religion does not change our character," (it may modify, may turn the curse into a blessing), " but the character of our unconverted state will be the character still of our converted life." If this be so, we cannot too early learn this virtue—this Fortitude—this power of holding on.

But we need to make acquaintance with her in another aspect just as early—to make acquaintance with her as THE POWER OF HOLDING BACK; for this, also, is her province and our need,—our need amid the many temptations with which we are beset. Strength of character is no protection for us here. Our strength is weakness. Many of the strongest characters in the world have been shivered to atoms and torn up by the roots, like forest trees before a furious tempest. You see them lying all about, broken, withered,—" whose end is to be burned." Just so you see men torn from their steadfastness, their work interrupted, their character marred, their life henceforth a maimed and worthless thing,—mere fuel, mere firewood. The strongest is weakness

B

itself in the hands of temptation.   Anyone can do right while it is easy, but only the soul fortified by principle and garrisoned by Christ can do right when it is hard. Can *you* do that?   Have you got that sterling stuff about you people call principle? Even if you have, I would not give much for it when some strong, subtle plot is laid against your virtue by Satan, unless in all and through all and above all be the mind of Christ and the might of Christ.

Tennyson writes about " The Talking Oak."   Well, if an oak could talk, it would be a small thing for it to say, " Here is a knot that came through the way I was bent by the wind, and yonder an incision made by some rough woodsman's axe."   Such would be merely the accent of sorrow, and would awaken your pity.   Rather differently would you feel if the tree told how some bird of prey came to build in his branches, and, after a little parleying, he welcomed it ; or how a serpent hatched its eggs and wound its coils round his trunk ; and how (worst of all, perhaps, because it seemed the least) a parasite plant dropped its seeds into his sap and sucked out his very life. Do my readers see what I mean? That circumstances are nothing—a strong man makes circumstances; and sorrows are nothing—a brave man bears sorrows; but sins, ah! sins are a very different matter; and unless we see their sinfulness, their exceeding sinfulness, and while forgiven the stain are delivered from the slavery; well—we shall continue slaves, that is all. We shall continue slaves in the vilest durance that ever was. It is mean, it is miserable, it is ruinous to body and soul; time cannot do with it, and eternity cannot endure, and yet must endure its presence. Surely, of all strength of character, the strength of character most to be coveted is strength against sin. And where shall we get it? "The strength of sin is the law." Strength against sin is the Gospel. "The glorious Gospel of the blessed God" announces and assures us of "delivering grace in the distressing hour." It is a telescope to show you Jesus at His Father's side. Father and Son are talking about you. What are they saying ? What *you* said to-day. " He is a miserable sinner, that man." Is that all they have to say ? I could have told that—did tell that myself. Nay, indeed, it is not all. " I will go down and deliver him." And if the man love Christ, He will love him and the Father will love him, and in the power of the Holy Spirit They will come unto him, and then when he returns to his house, instead of finding it empty, Satan finds it filled with the Spirit—full of God, that is ; and Satan says, I do not like God, and, though he does not choose to own it, he is afraid of God, too ; for Satan is a great coward. And so he goes away ; and thus the soul is nerved to patient continuance in well-doing, and the fiend is cast out by Fortitude which was put in by Christ.

But if Fortitude is to be ours, there must be not merely holding on and holding back, but HOLDING UP.

Sons and daughters of sorrow, " I desire to change my voice," and to speak in gentler tone when I speak to you.

Your temptations, it may be, are your trials. They are heavy, they are hard to bear ; long have they been borne by you, and you have need of Fortitude indeed to bear the strain of so much suffering, even an hour longer.

What shall I say to comfort you ? Shall I say, " We call them happy who endure," and "Whom the Lord loveth He chasteneth ?"

It is true, brother ; it is true, sister ; all quite true, and none the less because so familiar that we have hardly thought of it or applied it to ourselves. Take your trials as love tokens, and they will be, not bitter, surely, but very, very sweet. Shall I add that they "yield the peaceable fruit of righteousness." They tend to the moulding of character. Sweetbriar would not have its name, would not bear its roses either, were it without its thorns ; nor would life have half its loveliness without its sorrows.

It takes steel of the " ice brook's temper"

to make the sword the true soldier cares to wield, and your sorrows are the stream to temper the steel with which God Himself may sometimes fight. Those who shut themselves up from every breeze, and seek only in their wanderings the balmy air, never get braced, and seldom get strong, and souls that suffer no adversity are often found the frailest and seldom the fairest.

We see it in countries. In Russia, in Syria, in Egypt, many converts have been made; but how few have had fortitude to confess Christ, and how weak the Christianity of those countries in consequence. We see it in individuals. Those who never suffer are apt to be wanting in sympathy, wanting in humility,wanting in many things. So "we call them happy that endure." See that ye "endure hardness, as good soldiers of Jesus Christ."

For into this "building of God," "whose house are we," must be brought the "fir tree" (so straight), "the pine tree" (so true), and "the box " (so strong), "together, to beautify the place of " His " sanctuary."

Every noble and enduring quality of character must be cultivated, for the "house" to be built is so "magnifical," that we can afford to leave out none. I am quite sure you would like to find in all that serve and in any that love you ; to find in friends and dependents and relations, and especially in the nearest of all, something faithful, something firm. See to it that they also find it in you.

But how shall we do it, brethren ; how shall we do it ? By remembering that this is but *an addition.* Fortitude is not the first thing, the first thing is faith ; nay, if you will look at your revised version, you will see it is included in faith. That reads (in clumsy English, but very comforting theology) "in your faith supply virtue ; " in it, just as we read " all joy and peace in believing." So that "patient continuance in well doing," courage to meet temptation and calmness in trial, all, all are found in faith, for all are found in Christ in God, and having Him you have them. Yes, all in faith, but they are in it only potentially, like some unclaimed or unreclaimed lands are in some people's estates. Now it is our part to claim and to drain, and to make them productive, so shall they be ours actually too. Let us see to it that they are. Get the faith first, or rather get Christ by faith, and let it be the full Christ you get, and then look and see all you have gotten in getting Him, and amongst the all I am sure you will find Fortitude.

Weave' it then into the fabric of your life, and wear it under your armour in the battle, and wind it about you in the blast, so shall you be thrice blessed.

Yes, you who "holding on," are "not weary in well doing," shall "reap in due season if ye faint not," and "bringing your sheaves with you;" the "joy of harvest" shall be yours.

You, who, "holding back" from sin," fight the good fight of faith," bravely battling against evil, shall be crowned "more than conquerors through Him that loved" you; the joy of victory shall be yours.

And you, tried and suffering ones, yet

"holding up" under the storm of sorrow, and steadfastly enduring affliction; "though now for a season, if need be, ye are in heaviness through manifold temptations," soon shall you "receive the crown of life which the Lord hath promised to them that love Him;" and in the day when *He* is crowned, "in the day of the gladness of His heart," ye shall "enter into the joy of your Lord." And this shall be your "Welcome Home" —"To him that overcometh will I grant to sit with Me in My throne, even as I also overcame, and am set down with My Father in His throne."

PRUDENCE.

" Aristotle is praised for naming Fortitude the first of
the cardinal virtues, as that without which no other virtue
can steadily be practised ; but he might with equal
propriety have placed Prudence before it, since without
Prudence Fortitude is madness."

C. G. GOODRICH.

CHAP. II.

PRUDENCE.

"I wisdom dwell with prudence."—Prov. viii. 12.

AND a very good dwelling-place, too! Homely it is as can be, but that is a recommendation rather than a drawback; homely as the thatch that makes so picturesque a part of the landscape, or as the honeysuckle or woodbine that makes the house so bright and the porch so beautiful. Yes, Prudence is a homely home, but all the better for that.

Or shall we take it as the name, not of the habitation but of the inhabitant? If so, then Prudence is the careful house-mother, the thoughtful housewife, who makes both ends meet so well and all things work so smoothly—accustomed to accounts, and keeping them so well as to be a pattern to the whole parish, a sunbeam in joy, and when the clouds return after the rain, then the very bow in the cloud,—a delightful person altogether to live with. Happy the being who can say, like Wisdom, " I dwell with Prudence ! "

But who is Wisdom, Wisdom himself? Is he any other than Prudence under another name? I think he is. Greater things are said of him, much greater; so great that some have thought that Wisdom is not a personification but a person, that Person being the Word or Son of God— the Lord Jesus Christ. Probably, that is not so. Yet I think it evident that Wisdom is a larger, grander quality than Prudence. Though it is inclusive of that, it includes much more besides,—it includes Religion for one thing. But while it is greater, I grant, you must grant, in return, that it does not disdain it. Some people so represent (misrepresent, let us say) Religion that where religion begins common sense ends. Not so the Wisdom of Solomon, the Religion of God. This Wisdom, this Religion, so far from disdaining sagacity and undervaluing prudence, makes her a chosen companion, and says, " I dwell with Prudence."

Take Wisdom to represent Christ, and it means, I, Jesus, dwell where understanding dwells.

Take Wisdom to represent Religion, and it means, Religion comports with the highest self-love ; * and while it is good to remember for ourselves that not because of self-interest, but because of duty we are to be religious, it is good to remember for the honour of God and His Gospel that men are not made losers by Him for seeking it ; in the long run they will all be gainers —Wisdom dwells with Prudence.

---

* There is a right self-love, as well as a wrong selfishness. So moralists all but universally admit, and the Master affirms when He says :—" Love thy neighbour as thyself," thus implying that self ought to be loved.

In this, sacred and secular teachers are agreed, for when Sirach and Aristotle would make out the cardinal virtues, both placed it among them, and one of them assigned the first rank to this of PRUDENCE.

There are some who doubt its being held up as a virtue at all. " A mean, self-seeking, miserable, self-interested thing," they would tell you, " no one but Paley would praise it ; there is no place for it in any noble scheme of virtue." Well, I think if we were to pause in our speculation, to go out into the world and see there the havoc, the positive havoc that unwisdom, unthrift, and heedlessness occasion, we should have to say :—if prudence be not a virtue, it is quite certain that imprudence is a vice ; and if we dared to look down the jaws of hell and saw the souls of men lost to themselves and lost to God because devoid of understanding, we might come back with a better opinion of this homespun grace.　One proof—a negative one—that Prudence is a virtue.

Take another—one that is positive. The higher you ascend in the scale of being the more prudence is there manifested. A stone has none. A stock has none. And though some animals, some insects, have a great deal, it is all in a circle, however, round and round, with no progress in it. The bees in your agricultural shows, clever as they are, are not a whit more clever than the bees in the jaw bone where Samson found the honey. So the sagacity of a horse or a dog shows the lack of all progressive power. But man—man can use forethought, and can advance by using it. He knows more to-day than yesterday, more this century than last; witness the blaze of light that is preparing to turn night into day. Angels "excel in strength," and it is strength of mind, not body. "Are they not all—spirits?" And God—"God hath abounded toward us in all prudence." So the higher you ascend, the more of it do you find; and therefore, again, prudence is a virtue, and a leading one, a cardinal one.

Take one more reason, a scriptural one.

C

The Bible commands prudence and commends it. This book especially. It would be most interesting to go through the book of Proverbs with this thought,—What has Solomon written about prudence, how does God intend men to regard it? You would soon see that it is the "wise son who maketh a glad father;" that again and again, with all the affection of an impassioned parent, he urges him to plans and purposes and pursuits of sagacity and practical prudence. He reiterates it as if never tired of his lesson, and as if he never had done teaching it. To men, young men expressly, he cannot say too much about it.

And how speaks he of women in this matter? In an Eastern book, written in an age when women were not so esteemed as in our Western world and Christian centuries, it might hardly be expected that we should have reference to them in this matter at all. But what have we? Turn to the thirty-first chapter and read—" She seeketh wool and flax, and worketh willingly with her hands. She is like the merchant's ships, she bringeth her food from afar . . . She considereth [what prudence there! considereth] a field and buyeth it : with the fruit of her hands she planteth a vineyard. . . . She perceiveth that her merchandise is good : her candle goeth not out by night. . . She openeth her mouth with wisdom ; and in her tongue is the law of kindness. She looketh well to the ways of the household, and eateth not the bread of idleness." Really, very much of this description is a panegyric upon prudence ! Indeed the whole book runs in the same groove, so that it has been called " The Sanctification of Common Sense."

" But that was Old Testament virtue ; that was Solomon." Yes, it was Solomon ; that is, it was the wisest man who ever lived—a man, too, inspired of God. So to say advice is Solomon's is not to depreciate it much, I think.

But if you will not listen to the Old Testament, if you will not listen to Solomon, will you listen to the New Testament, will you listen to Christ ? In the New, I read about knowledge,—" To virtue knowledge," says St. Peter : about understanding,—" The spirit of power and of love, and of a. sound mind : " " Young men likewise exhort to be sober minded : " " The full assurance of understanding,"—and this is part of the work of that Being whose dispensation is the crown of the New Covenant—the Holy Ghost—by whom it is prayed for the Ephesians that " the eyes of their understanding may be enlightened," so writes St. Paul. I read in the Gospels themselves about the children of this world being— and it is said to their credit—" wiser than the children of light." The man who received the approval of Jesus in His most elaborate sermon is the " wise man who built his house upon a rock ; " and very earnestly does our Lord urge men to count the cost and exercise Prudence about the pearl of great price, and the purchase of the field and its treasure. So speaks the Master Himself. Yes, " The prudent are crowned with knowledge," and the crown is a " crown of life which the Lord, the righteous Judge will give in that day." We cannot undervalue Prudence unless we undervalue Christ.

I admit there is a wrong Prudence as well as a right. There is a selfish Prudence which always looks to the main chance, which follows Jesus because of the loaves, which always acts from interested motives. This is contemptible.

There is a wrong Prudence, too, which has the conceit of knowledge—a knowledge which puffeth up—which bloweth out the fancied possessor of it, like the frog in the fable. Such Prudence is beneath contempt. I do not say that you should practise that; but I do plead for that Prudence which Cicero defines as "the knowledge of what is to be desired and what is to be avoided;" which another speaks of as "an ability of judging what is best in the choice of both means and ends;" which yet another calls "a virtue of the soul; yea, the very soul of virtue,—the mistress to guide the life in goodness." I do plead for the use of the understanding, for that was what the great minds meant who placed Prudence among the cardinal virtues.

If God had not meant us to use our intellects, He would have made us without intellects; but as we are made, it is a peril to ourselves and a dishonour to Him to leave them unused. Solomon was right when He said—for indeed he said it from God, " Keep "—not throw away, not esteem lightly—" Keep sound wisdom and discretion."

Let us note some of the things in which this virtue may be exercised. It may be exercised *in temporal things, in spiritual things, and in eternal things.*

I have been partly led to treat this set of subjects by the observation, the very painful observation, of the way many people about us, old and young, men and women, manage their TEMPORAL concerns.

There are those who have been neglecting their business, caring nothing whether they have a balance at the banker's or a deficit; throwing about their money as if it were so much waste paper; making promises and breaking them, making professions and disgracing them, and altogether doing such wild work as makes sensible men weep. If the mischief stopped there, and the misery ended with themselves, we might let it pass and *only* weep ; but when we see that "one sinner destroyeth much good," that his bad actions affect a great many good people—then, we cannot cease to weep, but we cannot help also to blame, or at least to *warn*. And I do warn you. I will even say this, that *to neglect your business may be to neglect your God.* But I will not dwell on this, "a word to the wise ;" and if you are so foolish and so wicked as to disregard it, I fear no additional words of mine will have any weight. Do be warned in business and out of it, and like wisdom, "dwell with prudence."

I have spoken of money. I was going to speak of *marriage. Is there anything in which men and women are so imprudent—* if they were mere boys and girls they could hardly be more so ? Nay, some are imprudent in this matter upon principle.

They let themselves be carried away by their feelings, as if there were anything— any one thing—in which sound judgment illumined by the Spirit of God should so much be sought.

Health is another thing. I think as you look, in London especially, at the small forms and white faces of the men who are making the society of England, you cannot but feel that something, perhaps a good deal is wanting to make us a healthy nation ; nay, that it is almost impossible that work can be done as it should, or life lived as it might, with such attenuated frames. "You did not begin early enough," said a physician to a patient seeking health, "you should have begun two hundred years ago." Do you see his meaning ? So long, aye, and longer still, does one generation affect another.

But I pass from temporal to SPIRITUAL things, and I urge " the use of the understanding in matters of Religion." * I put

* See a paper under this title in Mr. Dale's admirable " Week-Day Sermons."

it to you—do you suppose that there would be the opposition to Religion there is in so many lands, and largely in this, if there had not been so much superstition ("pernicious nonsense" *The Times* called it) mixed up with the truth of God ? And do you suppose that there would have been this superstitious admixture if men had used their minds as they might ? Satan drugs the consciences of some men, he steals the senses of others. He says (I verily believe it) to your good men, many of them, " It does not matter much about your thinking right, so long as you feel right and do right."

Does it not ? Perhaps when you see coloured vestments and incense and ceremonies in their full-blown absurdity you will own that it *does* matter. Perhaps when you see how men of sense are revolted by the intolerably stupid superstitions and sentimental talk indulged in about sacramental grace and sacerdotal power, you will own that *right or wrong thinking may be as great a help or hindrance to the cause*

*of true religion and to the progress of it,
almost (I do not say altogether) as right or
wrong acting; and even more than right or
wrong feeling.*

Depend upon it, an intelligent race, like
the human race, must suffer if it has a non-
intelligent religion : in a multitude of cases
it will have no religion in consequence,
and so the light is first dimmed, and then
turned into darkness.

"If we would but be wise, we should
rarely fail to be virtuous," writes Rousseau,
and with some ground, surely.

But there is another, and perhaps equally
neglected use of prudence I want to point
out, and that is *in matters of temptation.*
"Fight wisely," insists Dean Goulbourn;
and what is it to fight wisely? I do not
remember just now what the Dean said.
I remember what His Master said : "He
that looketh upon a woman to lust after
her, hath committed adultery already in his
heart :" that is, the sin begins (He does not
say it is finished, He does not mean that
it is as bad—but it begins) long before the

act is committed. Then the way to stop its commission is to meet and manacle it where it begins.

Again, the Great Physician, going into this world of an Hospital Ward, puts His finger on the great patient lying there, and says : " Out of the heart,"—as if to say for all time, that is the source of the mischief, the seat of the disorder ; if the man is ever to be made healthy he must get a sound heart,—" Out of the heart proceed murders, adulteries, and such like."   Paul, too, says, " Make not provision for the flesh " (Rom. xiii. 14), one of the most important pieces of practical advice ever given, suggesting to the tempted one that *his duty and his safety lie in keeping out of the way of temptation.* To go into it, to make plans that might lead to it, is to stir up the " old lion," or the old Adam, rather, and to " make provision for the flesh."

Once more, so also is it in ETERNAL things.   Let me be frank with you, my readers.   There are some of you who claim to be prudent enough, who plume yourselves on your prudence even, who went all the way with me in what I said about indiscretion as to money and so on,—and even as to our seeking to have a religion animated, if not inspired, by common sense,—yet who, I fear, are lacking in this one particular ; and to be lacking here, my friends, is to have, not a cardinal virtue for the corner stone of character, but a cardinal vice.

For are there not, " are there not even among you," some who seek everything but the one thing,—everything but salvation and heaven, and can such expect to be exonerated when the question of Prudence is under discussion ?

You, prudent are you ? Let us see. You have been careful about your health ? Yes. And wealth ? Yes. You have looked into your affairs repeatedly ; but *you have a soul, and you are going to have an eternity? Where?* You do not know. And what about that soul ? You have not thought, or thought to purpose. The question is still an open question, whether it is saved or not at this moment. Is that prudent? Can you say it is? Do you think it is?

We read of a Roman, "a prudent man"[*] he was, in high office,—like one of our great Commissioners in India, I suppose,—and when the question of Christianity came up, he looked at it, and when he saw that it was true, he accepted it, he accepted Christ. Do you not think you ought to do the same ; as you value your soul, now do you not? That was Sergius Paulus. Well, you say, he lived a long time ago. Yes ; but it is as true to-day. "A prudent man looketh well to his goings." Do you? To your "going" to heaven or to hell.

In the train the other day, a gentleman I know well said to me : "Fifty years ago this month I went to a cottage meeting. The minister gave out his text, 'If thou hast run with the footmen.' I saw where I was running,—on the road to ruin, to destruction, and—I was eighteen at the time, but—I cried like a child. Next week the minister met me, and asked, 'If I had

---

[*] Acts xiii. 7.

ever been under concern for my soul?' I was overwhelmed, went to the woods to read and pray, and God brought me into liberty." Now, there was the exercise of Prudence. Many would have put away the conviction ; or, while letting it continue, would have gone on in the frivolities of youth, which were just then gaining an ascendancy over this young mind. Had he done so, he might have been lost—*lost for ever for want of* PRUDENCE.

It is most difficult for us, poor purblind beings that we are, to avoid being onesided. And I feel, as I re-read this chapter in praise of Prudence, that I would fain write another under Erasmus' title, "The praise of folly:" —such folly, I mean, as made men say that Paul was "beside" himself. Yes, I could wish to add a chapter on *disinterestedness*. For if the head is wrong, the heart is more wrong even than the head, and men not only act foolishly but do "very wickedly." One does long to sound in their ears, praying that it may echo in their consciences, such grand words as God's to Abram— "Walk before Me,* and be thou perfect." Surely half the faults of the world come from walking before men, instead of before God! Surely it would quicken and purify our life beyond expression were it lived as in the sight of the Lord, swayed and inspired by His consuming love! We all admire disinterestedness ; in God's name let us practise it.

---

* In the press,"Walk before Me : " Words for the New Year. By the Rev. J. B. Figgis.

# TEMPERANCE.

"Temperance is a bridle of gold, and he that can use
it aright is liker a god than a man."

BURTON.

CHAP. III.

TEMPERANCE.

"Every man that striveth for the mastery is temperate in all things."—1 *Cor. ix.* 25.

THE words transfer us to Trêves or Verona, Rome or Ephesus, and set us down in the midst of the games. There, in the arena, anon the scene of the torturing of wild beasts, and at other times of the martyrdom of Christians, a great contest now occupies the crowd. The racer, the rower, or it may be, the pugilist, strives for the mastery.

He runs, if in Greece, for the crown of laurel or parsley, if in the Roman world for some more substantial reward. Which-

D

ever it is, whatever the contest, whatever the crown, "he that striveth for the mastery is temperate in all things."

But is there not another scene, and another crown? Do not the suggestions of the text carry away our thoughts farther still, far as the gate of heaven itself, showing us there the claimants of everlasting glory?

For these, too, there are conditions of conquest.

The first of them is that they shall be in Christ, really, vitally, one with Him, so that His work is accepted for them ; but besides that there must be some harmony of character, some suitability of disposition, and this is to be won only by those who have attained to something of the virtue of temperance.

In taking up this, the third cardinal virtue, I ask my readers' special indulgence, for I feel the subject to be one of great delicacy, one too, calling for temperance of speech while treating of temperance in action. With more than usual prayerfulness should it be approached, both by writer and reader. In such a spirit, then, let us try to speak of this much needed virtue ; of its NATURE ; OF THE REASONS FOR ITS EXERCISE, AND OF THE REMEDIES FOR ITS DEFECTS : i.e., *of temperance, what it is, why it is to be sought, and how it is to be won.*

St. Paul before Felix " reasoned of temperance." " The fruit of the Spirit is . . . temperance." " Giving diligence we are to add to our faith—temperance." Now what is this temperance of which the Scripture is so fond, and what is its sphere ?

The word is used now-a-days of one particular form of abstinence, a very important form indeed ; considering the dangers seen and unseen around us, perhaps the most important, but still, Temperance—the word and the virtue—while they mean that, include other things beside. The word means government, control, it implies the putting forth of power, the exercise of force : it seems to say :—here is a place where you will have great need for exercising strength of character, see that you exercise it to the full. But where? Where, I say, does this King's writ run? What is the sphere of Temperance? It runs right round and right through all matters that have to do with the body; the appetites, the passions, the affections, all that we do, all that we feel, all that we desire.

Every one of these needs control. Every one of them is a racer that requires the rein, and the rein that is required is temperance. "He that striveth for the mastery is temperate in all things."

"In all things," not only in one thing, not even only in many. The universality of the principle is to me its strongest recommendation.

With all my heart do I rejoice in the blue wave that is breaking round our coasts. It was much needed. It may be a greater defence than that other wave, our "silver streak of sea." But let me remind those who are profoundly interested in this assault upon inebriety, that, urgently needed as it is, there are other matters demanding attention also. Without relaxing it in one direction, exert it in others. It is a blessed thing, I think, to have Gospel temperance, but—suffer the word of exhortation—do not make a Gospel of your temperance. If your heart is not right with God, all your temperance will not save you. Besides, this, as we have said, is but one form of temperance, and "He that striveth for the mastery is temperate IN ALL THINGS:" temperate in food, for Solomon says, "Put a knife to thy throat if thou be a man given to appetite;" temperate in drink, for Solomon adds, "Look not thou upon the wine when it is red, when it giveth its colour in the cup, when it moveth itself aright. At the last it biteth like a serpent and stingeth like an adder:" temperate in dress, for St. Peter urges to the garb of meekness, "the ornament of a meek and quiet spirit, which is, in the sight of God, of great price;" temperate in expenditure, learning to "be content with such things as ye have," and careful to "owe no man anything;" and even (yes, astonishing as it may seem) temperate in religion, for is it not written " Be not righteous overmuch ? " Some have tried to explain away that verse. Now, to my mind, it contains a most important principle ; this, namely, that church duties are not to be allowed to interfere with home duties, for to be praying when we ought to be working would be to be " righteous overmuch." It teaches, too, that we are not to be extravagant in our religion,— extreme or fanatical in our religion. Oh! from how much reproach religion would have been saved, if religious men had only remembered the warning, " Be not righteous overmuch ! " I am not counselling luke-warmness. God forbid. It is the last thing I would counsel. But I may, and do, urge you to that exercise of holy judgment which will make your religion a reasonable service. So wide, then ; so all embracing is this principle, Scripture is afraid of it in no department. It would cultivate in us a nature so balanced and large-hearted, and large-minded too, that all things would be shown to be touched by the highest influences.

But while the word is susceptible of so wide a meaning, the virtue respects chiefly a narrower range, and that range, as we have said, is ALL THAT BELONGS TO THE BODY. And surely here it has a very wide field for its exercise. The appetites and the passions ; surely their control is a matter worth attempting ; the appetites and the passions, would not their control be well nigh the reform of society ? The police would be set at liberty ; the law courts would have a perpetual long vacation; physicians and surgeons would have comparatively little to do. Healthy homes, happy homes, all but holy homes would smile upon us on all sides. And though that exception, that 'all but,' is a very great one, yet, for it too, help would be found in the removal of two of the greatest hindrances to the Gospel :—incontinence, and excess of wine. So that, every one that loves his country, that loves his fellow-men, must long, and pray, and strive for the progress of the principles and practice of this cardinal virtue of Temperance.

REASONS for seeking the promotion of this virtue lie around us on every side. It is for the honour of God. THE SPHERE OF TEMPERANCE IS THE BODY, AND THE BODY IS A TEMPLE. I cannot, indeed, with Robertson, say to the unrenewed man, "*your* body is the temple of the Holy Ghost;" but I can say, it might have been: it ought to be. It has been desecrated, nay rather, it has never been consecrated; it is not a temple, but every stone is there :—the abilities, the faculties, the feelings, all that might make it a temple: and God, the God whose presence would be the act of consecration, whose coming would be the consecrating hour, "He is not far from every one of us."

What would you say to one who should bring pollution into some building, made or meant for holy purposes? What did the Jews say when they supposed St. Paul had brought Greeks into the temple? What have Englishmen said about soldiers

stabling their horses within Cathedral walls?
How much more may men complain—and
God condemn — if any have brought
polluting thoughts, polluting acts, a polluting
atmosphere into that which God made or
meant to be so pure!

I referred to Robertson just now, and
had to express some divergence from his
opinion ; but I wish, I wish right heartily,
that the manhood of England and of the
world, could get his love of purity, his
reverence for woman ; so that, in word,
deed, thought, no sullying thing even was
allowed to tarry in his mind on such subjects. Oh ! seek, seek to be pure. A body
tainted by lust is like a temple occupied by
bandits ; and what is a body filled with
strong drink, but a temple " set on fire of
hell ? " Surely the demons of the pit must
rejoice at such a sight ; nay, the demons of
the pit have caused it. Well may the son
of Sirach say : " Show not thy valiantness
in wine, for wine hath destroyed many."
And as well : " Go not after thy lusts but
refrain thyself from their appetites. If

thou givest thy soul the desires that please her, she will make thee a laughing-stock to thine enemies. Take not pleasure in much good cheer, neither be tied to the expense thereof. Be not made a beggar by banqueting upon borrowing, when thou hast nothing in thy purse ; for thou shalt lie in wait for thine own life, and be talked on." And in better known and heaven-sent words, we may say of each vice in question, " She hath cast down many wounded, yea, many strong men."

"Strong men " indeed ! There was the greatest conqueror of the Grecian world, the man whose empire spread from Macedonia to India, who planned Alexandria and conquered Babylon. Whence, one day, issued in long procession a vast retinue of retainers, of officers, of captive kings. Wherefore their march, and whither ? To Alexandria, to lay there that coffin of gold, drawn by those sixty-four mules, and bearing within it all that was mortal of the great Alexander. Yes, the conqueror has been conquered at last ; and the cause of his defeat, the cause of his early death, is said to have been the love of wine.

"Strong men" assuredly! There was the hope of Protestantism, the hero of Chivalry, the darling of France; so brave, so generous, full of every fascination as a man, of every royal virtue as a king, yet Henry of Navarre was the dupe of every passing beauty, the slave of his own lust.

And if the strong men fail, how shall the weak ones stand?

Be warned, be wise in time. Be "temperate in all things;" for the sake of your intellect; quite impossible will it be to keep it clear, if the body be pampered with viands, inflamed with lust, or excited by wine; for the sake of your spiritual powers, which must grovel in the dust the moment such a life is yielded to; and for the sake of the very part of your nature, you would gratify and degrade. "Every sin that a man committeth is without the body, but he that" indulgeth lust or love of wine "sinneth against the body."

Nor think merely of the harm it will do

you, but of the harm YOU *will do.* One longs to see a healthy race inhabiting the earth, but our base-born desires propagate feebleness and promote frailty. Example, too, affects, and some directly drag others into sin. Instead of this, "live Christ," transmit health, promote purity, be centres of self-restraint and respect.

"God is not in all their thoughts," who banish temperance from their lives. But God should be, and that even in things the least and the lowest. "Whether, therefore, ye eat or drink, or whatsoever ye do, do all to the glory of God."

"The body is for the Lord and" (more blessed still), "the Lord for the body." So that we should strive to serve Him by whom we are so fearfully and wonderfully made, and we may hope to do so. God helping us ; "His glory" may yet be written in the very members of our material frame.

That we may do this, may help others in a similar course of well-doing, we must be ready to use the REMEDIES required by the evils against which we are contending.

The evils, and perhaps especially the evils in the matter of inebriety, are fourfold— moral, religious, physical, and social; the remedies must be fourfold likewise. This is sometimes forgotten or denied. That they must be moral, all men, that they must be religious, all religious men, will admit. Religion is the mainspring, and morals are the jewels of this precious mechanism which we would have keeping time with the great dial of God, and that uninterruptedly to all eternity. So far we are agreed. Perhaps even most will allow that physical evils need physical remedies. "Whatsoever a man soweth that shall he also reap." When one tastes the winecup, it has been strikingly said, a seed is sown in the appetite, and it is natural that it should grow, and bring forth fruit after its kind. In a certain per-centage of persons it will lead to liking, then to loving, and afterwards to living for the sin. This craving can only be conquered by absolute avoidance. Here, too, agreement is general. But we divide into two separate (not hostile) camps when we proceed to advocate the social and physical remedies.

As to the social remedy, we say wine is the occasion of falling. Cut off the occasion, and we are answered—you are seeking to be wiser than God and kinder than Christ. Our reply might be, do you not try to screen your sons from scenes of lust; are there not evils " not so much as named amongst you as becometh saints?" And why should not the same course be taken, why should it not be right, why should it not be successful in the matter of intemperance as well as of incontinence? But we prefer to put it thus. A few years ago, we can suppose a slave-holder in defence of his " peculiar institution " saying, Christ was not an abolitionist, and adducing the example of St. Paul as enjoining obedience upon slaves. The statements would have been true in *the letter* of them, but the whole Spirit of Christ and of Christianity is—as we all feel now—adverse to that " sum of all villainies," the holding men as chattels. Now here is proof positive that there may be a growth in Christian morality. No one doubts now that the abolition of slavery is pleasing to Christ, and why should not this assault upon this other slavery be pleasing too? The Spirit of Christianity is the very spirit of the best-based total abstinence ; for the spirit of both is self-sacrifice for the sake of others.

"But you cannot make men virtuous by act of parliament." I am speaking of social customs and personal influence, not of acts of parliament at all : though if I were, I might contend with so calm and dignified a disputant as Dr. Alexander Raleigh, that, " Acts of parliament when they are wise and suitable to the people for whom they are framed, do help instrumentally to make men virtuous, and when they are unwise and evil, to make men vicious. The State can refuse to tempt or to sanction temptation. In one word, we have it on the highest authority, she can be as the minister of God for good."

And what the State can do in her great place, that, in our little place, can we. The question is, Are we doing it ? As units in the nation, we are responsible, in some faint measure, for the laws of the nation ; as individuals in society, we are more largely responsible for influence in our individual circle. Is that influence for Temperance always ? "Yes," say my readers one and all, "for Temperance, certainly ; we do not all say for total abstinence." I will not argue the point with you, I will only mention a case that comes painfully home to myself :—a case of terrible inebriety in one refined, cultured, once hopefully converted to God. One who had spent long care and prayer, with no sparing of pains or cost, said this about the awful condition [perdition ?] of the fallen one : " What strikes me is that all this had a beginning." Yes, it " had a beginning ; " and the beginning was, not in the debauch of the drunkard, but in the sip Society sanctions and smiles on. Surely, if we be men, much more if we be Christians, another thing will strike us, this, namely,— that it would be good to prevent the "beginning," very good to adopt and promote such social habits as shall take away the occasion of falling. This, at least, is what strikes *me*.

But I forbear. Indeed, I had not become aware that this subject must come under notice till after undertaking to treat of the cardinal virtues. But, as it has come up, I cannot honestly withhold my opinions, I can only seek to manifest temperance in declaring them.

This, further, I feel it laid upon my heart to say: Come with us; it will do you no harm to come, two thousand physicians guarantee that. "Come with us and we will do you good." For, if there be some self-denial, is it not good to deny ourselves for others' sake, for others' safety? If not a universal need,—and with the example of Christ and the existence of vineyards, I am not prepared to say that it is,—yet is it not "good for the present distress?" A Spartan remedy, perhaps, but a successful one for an evil desperate and deplored by all. I say "successful," for stop recruiting

E

and the army in time will fail.   Stop the
supply of drunkards, and " the devil's army
of the line" will pass with a passing
generation.   Prevention is better, safer,
and easier than cure, therefore we go in for
prevention.   You have seen many live
dishonoured and die disgraced, because of
excess of wine.   What are you going to do
to check it ?   In God's name, do something.

We do not judge you who do not see
with us that abstinence is the best remedy.
God forbid that we should judge any man's
servant ; we have enough to answer for our
own sin.   But we beg of you this : If you
cannot join our ranks, cheer and help those
who do, for we know you rejoice with us
in the diminution of excess, and you do
wish us well.   If you cannot come with us
the whole way, come as far as you can ;
say, like a young man I know,—" I am a
man of one glass," and never touch a
second.   Or if you shrink from the full
temperance pledge, take some other like
that the Sovereign signed, it is said, early
in her reign, thousands of her subjects

joining her, to abstain from all kinds of ardent spirits. If we must be in separate, let us at least be in friendly camps, and in full alliance. Temperance, we are all agreed, is good. Let us practise it ; let us promote it ; let us introduce substitutes for the cup of danger as constantly and completely as we individually can. So let us seek, as parents, as pastors, as friends, as Christians, to be " temperate in all things." I repeat the word and emphasize it, *all* things. No one shall run a tilt against me for sparing gluttony while I oppose drunkenness, or for being apathetic about purity while seeking to promote sobriety. I hope none of us are so intemperate as that. I pray that we may all be worthy to be countrymen of Andrew Marvell, and by simplicity of living in *every* way, " let ' our ' moderation be known unto all men." " Consider what I say, and the Lord give you a right judgment in all things."

I wish I could hope to say something to

the purpose on the other class of temptations to which man is exposed in regard to "the temple of his body." The difficulty of dealing with it is so great, as to leave people almost without human guidance in matters in which they need guidance most.

Perhaps that will be no harm to us if we are all the more thrown upon God, and go to Him to learn all that may make and keep us pure. And assuredly He has not left us without a witness. There are in that book of the Bible, which contains the essence of the most profound, practical wisdom—the Book of Proverbs—chapters in the earlier part which are an invaluable directory, especially for young men. Then, St. Paul gives a hint of the only hope of our elevation above impurity, — a chivalrous regard for the rights of others, —in a sentence obscured in the Authorized Version, but more clearly represented in the Revised Version. It is in 1 Thess. v. 6, where, having spoken of adultery and concupiscence, St. Paul goes on to say, " That no man defraud or go beyond his brother

IN THE MATTER, because that the Lord is the avenger of all such. . . . For God hath not called us unto uncleanness, but unto holiness." This draws attention off ourselves, from the harm we are likely to receive, and fixes it on others (on the husband, in the case of adultery), and the wrong we are likely to inflict. This is the right order ; and he who dwells upon it must be mean indeed, who, after that, can persist in such a sin.

Do not the Master's own words cover a like possibility of baseness when He says : " Whosoever causeth one of these little ones to offend, it were better for him that a mill-stone were hanged about his neck, and that he were cast into the depths of the sea ? "

This to regulate our thought of others, and "he that looketh" lusts, to regulate our own thought, form directions plain enough for all but the wilfully blind.*

---

* Those who feel that they need details as well as principles on these subjects, may with advantage consult St. Francis de Sales' " Devout Life," and Bishop Jeremy Taylor's " Holy Living."

The sum is this, that the body as being God's, is to be as much and as wholly used for God, as any other part of man's being. How to bring about such divine use of it, in himself and in others—" that we may glorify God in our body "—is surely a purpose every way worthy of the concern of every Christian, as it is the duty of every man. A help to the desired end would be the creating and cherishing a spirit of purity as much above mere abstinence from outward evil, as true honour is superior to bare honesty. We want woman's influence in this reform as well as the other. One thing all women can do : let them never speak as if that was to be expected in their brothers and male friends which would not be tolerated in themselves. I shall never forget hearing a bright young girl, an heiress too, say, some twenty years ago now, " I do rather like fast men." Alas ! alas ! for manhood, if womanhood thinks thus. Instead of this, every girl should be a vestal virgin to guard the holy fire of the nation's purity.

But after all, our hope is in God. The heart needs to be changed, to be cleansed, and to be kept clean, and only One Fountain can do this.

Let God put His hand upon the rein, and the racer will stop. Not else. "The fruit OF THE SPIRIT is temperance." If, and in proportion as we are imbued with that Spirit, we shall be "temperate in all things:" in speech, guarded and generous; in opinion, well-balanced and rational; in expenditure, modest and moderate; in food and drink, simple ; self-denying, thoughtful for others ; and still more thoughtful lest we "go beyond or defraud any in the matter" of purity and holy love.

We must look to God to cleanse His temple, and then the whole house—even "the earthly house of this tabernacle "— will be filled with His Glory.

JUSTICE.

"Justice is a great deal more difficult than Mercy to find and rarer . . . Fear God and have no other fear. Serve God and every other service will sink into its right proportions, 'for one is your Master, even Christ, and all ye are brethren.'"

From " PLAIN SPEAKING."

CHAP. IV.

JUSTICE.

OF all the cardinal virtues commend me to the virtue of justice. The others are virtues for self, this is a virtue for society. The others are virtues to help a man to live happily, this is a virtue to help a man to live righteously. Indeed, justice is almost another name for righteousness; and, as that includes all that is right, this cardinal virtue may be taken as inclusive of every right thing, as nearly equivalent to virtue itself. So the great Stagirite defines it,— "What is justice?" he asks; and he answers, "To give every man his own." If it has regard to every man, then indeed, is it a broad stone of honour, and if it consists in giving him his own, then is it assuredly something demanded, for *to keep that which is another's, is to be a thief.* But even this is too restricted. Why only men? Why not every being? Every angel, every animal has his rights; and so, above all, God Himself. "Will a man rob God?" Can that be justice which takes no account of HIM? Assuredly he only is just who gives to every being, and to God, first, that which is his own.

You see, then, from the very definition of it, the supreme concern of our present subject, the immense importance of justice. And yet how unimportant it seems to some men! There are those who would not drink, or swear; would give way neither to lust nor crime; nay, who seek truth, and, perhaps, plume themselves upon it; who love holiness, even, and go a long way to seek it, who yet think little or nothing of doing a man, or a whole body of men; of doing a nation, or a whole group of nationalities, grievous injustice. Either they do not see injustice to be a sin, or they do not see their conduct to be an injustice. I have heard people of excellent character, of religious character, say and do things which pressed and trenched on the rights of others ; and they not only did not see the sin of it, they thought they were doing a good and holy thing.

But to hold up truth by unrighteousness, is to sin against justice, and that can never serve truth.

Now in opposition to all this, which history tells us has been going on since the world was ; and we, if we do not take care may make such history :—in opposition to this, I long, by God's grace, to see in my family first, in my friends next, in my flock, and in all in any way under my influence, an intense and imperishable love of justice ; so that no one of us shall ever do or say or think any thing unjust of any persons, or class of persons ; shall ever do or be a party to any religious, any social, any political movement, which produces or perpetuates an injustice. We may not be clever, we cannot be rich, but at least let us be just. That surely is a character which each of us may hope to win and to wear, and I pray God that we may so live that no one may ever ask, or have any right to ask of anything that we do, "Is it just?" Yes, may live so as to deserve to have written on our graves, "a just man."

In order to this we must understand something of the importance of justice, and the instruments of justice.

God *commendeth* justice, speaking of Joseph the husband of Mary as "a just man;" of Simeon, as "a just man and devout;" of John the Baptist, as "a just man and holy;" of Joseph of Arimathea, and of Cornelius, each as "a just man." The God of the Bible evidently looks to find this character in men whom He delighteth to honour.

God *commandeth* justice: in kings, saying, "He that ruleth over men must be just, ruling in the fear of God;"—in buyers and sellers, saying, "Just balances, just weights, a just ephah, and a just hin, shall ye have," "thou shalt have a perfect and just weight, a perfect and just measure shalt thou have;"—"execute judgment and justice, take away your exactions from my people, saith the Lord God. Ye shall have just balances, and a just ephah, and a just bath." Jesus answered John, "thus it becometh us to fulfil all righteousness." Paul before Felix, "reasoned of righteousness." And to all His people God says, " Keep ye equity, and do justice."

God *promiseth* to bless the habitation of the just; and again, "blessings are upon the head of the just;" and again, "a just man falleth seven times and riseth again;" "the just shall come out of trouble;" "the tongue of the just is as a chain of silver;" and, more strikingly still, "the wealth of the sinner is laid up for the just." As for happiness or honour, a wicked man "may prepare it, but the just shall put it on." So Scripture throughout insists on this most essential virtue.

And I find a law in my conscience agreeing with this in my Bible. I find there

a reason and reward for all virtues, but
a double one for this. I feel a sense of
duty to do all the good I can, in all the
ways I can, to all the people I can, but
a double duty to give unto all that which
is just.

Of course in proportion as a man is good
and generous, noble and large-hearted, he
will feel about anything that is good, that
he is a debtor till he shares it with others.
So St. Paul felt about the gospel, and so
St. John felt about what he had seen and
heard of the Word of Life ; that he would
be selfish unless he sought that others also
might have fellowship with him. But
though that was a debt for St. Paul, I put
it to you, was it as fully a debt as some lia-
bility he had incurred in his tent making ?
Though that was a duty for St. John, was
it as primary a duty as that he should
render to Zebedee and Salome and James,
that which was their own ? Surely the one
was a kind act, to omit which was to sin
against the law of grace, but the other
a righteous act, to omit which was to sin

against the law of nature too. I find it very hard to put my meaning into words, lest one should seem to give countenance to the idea of supererogation. But I have a profound conviction that justice is the primary virtue, and that it rests on a stronger ground of necessity than kindness, or pity, or the like. The one I take to be the filling, the other the overflowing of the pitcher, and the filling must come first.

The tenants of a friend about to be married—he has property in Ireland—wanted to give him a present; but they were "boycotted," and could not. "Well," he says, "I do not want the present, I want my rents." So I suspect we all feel in similar circumstances, that many things that may be done are very delightful, they are unexpected, and can never be demanded; but justice we have a right to expect, and may demand. And if so, remember people may demand it of you, and to withhold it is grievously to sin.

I have referred to Ireland,—even before late troubles, one weak point in the cha-

F

racter of its people was, that they very often forgot to be just before they were generous. A warning this not to be forgotten !

If justice be a virtue, and the foundation of all virtues, then injustice must be a vice, and a very great vice. I beseech you to think it nothing less : not to think him a vicious man who lets his appetites master him, but him virtuous who is only mastered by selfishness. To do another, and especially to do whole classes of men and of interests, an injustice, is one of the greatest of vices. I wish I were as sure you would all believe and act on this, as I am that it is true.

But I want to bring you back to your Bibles again, and to get you to notice what your Bibles say about God Himself, and how they represent Him in this matter. This is important and interesting every way, because you know that many nations have had gods utterly and flagrantly unjust ; but very early in Scripture Abraham, who was God's pupil in the solitudes, showed that he had got the true apprehension about the Deity in this matter, for he says, " Shall not the Judge of all the earth do right ? " So had Moses when he said, " The Lord shall judge His people." And God Himself says no less, for He proclaims Himself by Isaiah, " A just God and a Saviour ; " and He is jealous of His character for justice, for when the views of things were getting confused, He asks by Ezekiel, " Are not My ways equal ? " Yes ; the justice of God is incontestable and immutable, and if ever we are to be " imitators of God as dear children," we must be just, too ; aye, and that at all costs.

For you remember when the question came up, as it had to come up,—how the just God could justify the ungodly, that for answer God arose out of His place, and went out of his way to find—nay, to be—the ransom and the righteousness of the ungodly : that having lived for them, and for them having died, their restoration might be a possible and practicable thing. Yes, His justice to the universe cost God

Christ, and Calvary; and I ask you in sight of that bleeding victim, God-offered and God-accepted, how much store think you must God lay by such an attribute, how intensely must such a God love righteousness and justice, and hate injustice? While all who strive after justice may be sure of His smile, all who are guilty of injustice have cause indeed to tremble at His frown.

But again. Turn from God the Infinite to God Incarnate. Who and what is He? Stephen calls Him "that Just One;" Ananias speaks of seeing "that Just One;" James charges the rich,—"Ye have slain the just;" Paul tells all, "He died the Just for the unjust." The Just, the Just One, it is another name for Jesus then! Pilate had said, "I am clear from the blood of that Just Person," and Pilate's wife advises him to have "nothing to do with that Just man," the centurion says "surely this was a righteous man." If we would be Christ-like we must be righteous men, not merely believing men, kind men, loving men, praying men, heavenly-minded men; all this, yes,—but over and above all, righteous men, just men ; *i.e.*, men who do righteous acts, who live just lives, with whom righteousness and justice are a habit and a practice.

This might lead us to speak of the *sphere* of justice ; but I must note yet another proof of its importance first. Everybody that understands anything of mathematics or geometry, knows that an angle is of the same value whether we take it near the apex or when the sides have been produced ever so far, and the angle has become ever so wide. If it is an angle of 15 at the one point, it is an angle of 15 at the other ; or, if it is an angle of 45 at the one point, it is an angle of 45 at the other ; although it does not look nearly as large. Now, it is so also with our moral acts, *e.g.*, our acts of injustice, they look very small perhaps at first, but may be very large in God's sight, for He sees to what they may reach. Take, for instance, the disabilities of the Jews. These seemed to some a small thing ; they could not see the injustice of refusing them a seat in Parliament. But—while some-

thing must be allowed to excited feeling
against usury—is it not the same spirit
intensified that has led to the frightful
outrages against Israel in Russia, which
have saddened so many hearts? So with
other persecutions : people see that it was
wrong for Philip II. to issue those terrible
edicts which have made infamous the Blood
Council in the Netherlands ; but they fail
to see the wrong done to thousands of their
fellow-countrymen by the withholding from
them their share in national honours and
emoluments. In reality, however, disabilities
and persecutions are only different degrees
of the same wrong, and neither of them, I
am sure, could ever have been allowed if
all law-makers in all ages had had in their
hearts a full sense of justice. I think if I
were a conforming, instead of a " noncon-
forming member of the Church of England,"
I could never rest day nor night till the
last vestige of equality and disability, *i.e.*,
of injustice, were removed from the statutes
of the land and the canons of the church.
It is not a question of what I can assent

to merely, but of whether it is right to put up barriers that do bar the way to some who may have as good a right to pass as I. All laws that do this, contravene that first principle of giving every man that which is his own. Persecution had never been, slavery had never been, war (I almost suspect) had never been, if there had been broad and deep the river of justice flowing in the hearts of men. The terrible, tremendous cruelties and calamities that have fallen on the world prove that it is a grievous and bitter thing to be unjust, that it leads to infinite misery and mischief in the end thereof. Roman Catholics are not the only people who do evil that good may come ; but I would have you note well that holiness, truth, right, are never advanced by that which is unjust to any ; for *injustice always leaves a sting which would hinder the reception of good, and (if not) a stain which would hinder the communication of it.*

Justice is an imperial virtue, and has a dominion on which the sun never sets.

She is the queen of public morality and of private morality, too ; the very arbitress of the dealings of man with man. She is the handmaid of religion, the coping-stone of divine theology. Do we speak of *social* justice ? Justice, like charity, begins at home. Justice binds together families, teaching what is due from husband to wife, from parent to child, from brother to sister. It is the fundamental virtue of social life. I admit there are various interests, but they are not clashing interests. God can beautifully adjust them all, and so arrange that each shall have his own. Indeed, that can be no justice to one which is an injustice to another, for justice is what is due ; justice is for each to have his own, not what is another's.

Do we speak of *political* justice ? I should like to tell our historians they need it in writing history ; our legislators, that they need it in making laws ; our voters, that they need it in sending men into the senate. I should like to see all evince justice. You want it when you go to exercise your right as citizens, when you take up a book, when you read the newspaper. Belong to that party in the state which seems to you most instinct with love, or, at least, with justice; to that church or denomination which best carries out the maxims of holy justice. Surely this is better than to be led by our feelings, our tastes, our prejudices, or our passions,

Nor must I omit *commercial* justice. God does not. "Ye shall do no injustice in judgment, in meteyard, in weight, or in measure." "Thou shalt not have, in thy bag divers weights, great and small. Thou shalt not have in thy house divers measures, great and small. But thou shalt have a perfect and just weight, a perfect and just measure shalt thou have."* "It is more possible now to cheat in the quality than in the quantity of the article. Dishonesty of every kind is an abomination to the Lord. Justice is His delight, alike in the weight of the goods, and in their worth."†

---

* Deut. xxv. 13.   † Arnot.

One who was perfectly just would be perfectly good. One who was really just would fail in no duty to any being.

Our last and most difficult inquiry concerns THE WAY OF ATTAINING TO JUSTICE— the way to be just. Job asked, " How should man be just with God ? " A difficult question that to answer,—a tremendous question. It had to be answered amid agony and blood, darkness and desolation, the scourge and cross, Gethsemane and Calvary. It took the death of God's Son to answer it. He is our righteousness; the claims of justice were all met in Him. Dr. Beaumont puts it strikingly, if strongly, when he says :—" When the Man Who was God's Fellow came ; then came the most terrible cry ever heard in the universe. Awake ! O sword, smite the Shepherd. It smote Him, in Bethlehem, it smote Him all along the highway of life. On Calvary the stroke of the sword darkened the sun, shook earth, shook hell. It only fell when He fell, and then the sword of justice lay at the foot of the cross, hushed, lulled, pacified ; it lay there till the third hallowed morning, when it was found changed into the sceptre of mercy, and that sceptre of mercy has been waving among mankind ever since."

But there is another question. " How shall a man be just with" *man ?* For surely this should be ; yet who that knows anything of life and duty but must feel how hard it is to fill every relationship, every vessel to the full ; to render to all their dues. For this we feel that we want, not a substitute, but a supply ; not an expiation for the omission of duty, but an inspiration for the accomplishment of it. How shall we get this inspiration ? Where shall we find this supply ? Where strike the precious lode of ore that shall make us perfectly upright, transparently sincere, equable, uniformly kind, indulgent, tenderly loving, perfectly pure, and perfectly patient —" patient towards all men ? " Where shall we get the grace of Justice, that, instead of going into the social atmosphere, even

the religious atmosphere most agreeable,—
aye, as we think, most helpful,—we shall
keep always and only in that which our
consciences approve,—with the weak, the
despised, the forsaken, if duty points to
them? Where get the equity which shall
never trench on another's rights, never push
the noblest cause by ignoble measures;
never move or stir save where the compass
of justice points?

For this we need the *principles of justice,*
that is to say, we need to be conscientious
about being just, to make a conscience of it,
to be as inflexible about it as Aristides or
Fabricius. But principle is not enough.
Men want power, want motive, want motive
power—that is to say, moving power. Now,
the most moving power, the strongest
motive in the world, is LOVE. That man
will be most just whom the love of Christ
constraineth best. He will say to himself,
"My Master loved justice, was incapable
of injustice ; and that, even when being
just ruined (to all appearances) His cause
cost Him His happiness, His ease, His

life." Jesus did not disdain despised minorities. He was once in a minority of one, for His disciples (Peter being their spokesman) would have had Him give way. A minority of One, or of two (shall we say?) God His Father being one of the two, and therefore, notwithstanding all, Christ came off triumphant.

There is only one thing better than the love of Christ, and that is THE CHRIST HIMSELF. To be swayed by His love is happiness, to be possessed, mastered, in-dwelt by His Spirit is holiness, and that holiness we may have ; for Christ " is made of God unto us sanctification," and when we have it, then, and not till then, we shall be holy too ; we shall be perfectly just.

So the way to be just is to get that Just One. Yes, Jesus is " the Way."

Friends, we are getting nearer the judgment seat. That there is a throne of justice in the universe, present inequalities, sorrows, and sins unequally adjusted here, palpably prove. There is a throne of

justice, but how shall we face it? How
stand at its bar? Have we been just to
parents, children, wife, servants, friends,
God? Aristides may face that bar. I
cannot say as to Aristides, for I do not
know his heart, and I do know that he had
less opportunity. He did not know my
Jesus. But if he can face it, I cannot. "I
cannot answer thee one of a thousand,"
but Christ can. Therefore would I creep
into Christ and shelter myself there for
ever.

Yet, even this—this atonement and inter-
cession of "Jesus Christ the righteous,"*—
is no salve for me if I persist in any course
or act of injustice. The edict of God to
me is that I "sin not,"—that comes first,—
that I "render, therefore, to all their dues."
The Lord God requires of me "to do
justly and to love mercy," as well as to
walk humbly with my God. And only
when I strive to do so am I drinking into
the Spirit of Jesus. "He that doeth

* 1 John ii. 1.

righteousness is righteous, even as He is righteous." *He that would have part and lot in that Just One* MUST BE JUST.

Reader, whoever thou art, who has perused my halting description of these cardinal, these right royal, virtues, do not be content with reading it and with praising them. It is not panegyric, but practice, that God wants. Go and show *fortitude* under thy daily crosses or losses. Go and practice *prudence* in thy every duty, from the reception of theological truth to the regulation of household expenditure. Practise *temperance*, too, sweet unsullied temperance "in all things :" while, as to *justice*—believe me it will be a happy day for you when you fall in love with justice ! In every transaction, in every religious or political combination, in every dealing with men, in every duty to God, see to it that whatever you are not, you are always and altogether *inflexibly and unalterably just.*

So "giving all diligence"* to "add to your faith" this and every virtue, "ye shall neither be barren nor unfruitful in the knowledge of our Lord Jesus Christ.†" He is the soul's one and only foundation, but let us build on Him "gold, silver, precious stones"—FORTITUDE, PRUDENCE, TEMPERANCE, JUSTICE.

*2 Peter i. 5.   †2 Peter i. 8.

D. B. FRIEND, PUBLISHER AND PRINTER, BRIGHTON.

WORKS BY THE REV. J. B. FIGGIS
(Continued).

"LESSONS LEARNT IN ITALY AND THE RIVIERA."

Crown 8vo. 208 pp., cloth, 3s.

By the REV. J. B. FIGGIS, M.A.,

Minister of the Countess of Huntingdon's Church, Brighton.

ALSO a Special Large Paper Edition, printed on Crown 4to., toned paper, and illustrated by **TWELVE BEAUTIFUL PHOTOGRAPHS**, by Signor Brogi, of Florence. Bound in handsome cloth, gilt, bevelled edges, price 21s.

D. B. FRIEND has had a few copies put into elegant Calf and Morocco bindings by SUTTABY & Co., of London, and are especially suitable for Wedding and other presents.

REVIEWS.

"Mr. Figgis has turned to excellent account the incidents of what was a most pleasant and healthful journey. His descriptions of Pompeii, Pæstum, Rome, and Assisi, are particularly interesting; he gathers up out-of-the-way facts now and then, and makes good use of them. In the chapters on Rome we have the results of some reading in the best kind of literature, classical and modern, and all is made to throw light on Scripture allusion. This is indeed, in one respect, the strong point of Mr. Figgis's book."—*British Quarterly*.

"We give it our hearty commendation. There is not a dull or prosy sentence in the volume, and it must benefit mind and heart."—*Evangelical Magazine*.

77, WESTERN ROAD, BRIGHTON.

Hidden Life: Memorials of JOHN WHITMORE WINSLOW. By his Father, OCTAVIUS WINSLOW, D.D. Eighth Thousand. Fcap. 8vo. With Portrait. 3s. 6d., Cloth. "We are not surprised at this book being still in demand. It is the life story of a son of whom a father might well be proud. . . . We heartily commend this memorial to all our readers."—*Christian.*

SECOND EDITION.

The Last Sermon preached by the late REV. OCTAVIUS WINSLOW, D.D. Together with the FUNERAL SERMON, by the REV. E. L. ROXBY, M.A., Incumbent of St. Margaret's, Brighton. To which are added Memorial Verses—"The Great Uplifting." Fcap. 8vo. 6d., sewn.

A Bible Calendar for Young People. Designed to encourage the habit of daily perusing the Scriptures. By WILLIAM OLDING. Fourth Edition. Cloth, 6d. ; paper, 3d.

The Return of the Jews to the Holy Land. Being a collection of thoughts in verse on the return of the Jews to their long-lost home. In Memoriam, by J. B. Cloth, Ninepence.

Your Election of God. By the REV. J. G. GREGORY, M.A., Incumbent of Emmanuel Church, Hove, Brighton. Published by request. Price Fourpence.

ALSO BY THE SAME AUTHOR.

No Priests of God Upon Earth, Independently of the entire body of Christ. Price Fourpence.

Private Prayer. By the REV. JAMES VAUGHAN, M.A., Incumbent of Christ Church, Brighton. Published by request. Price One Penny.

No More Remembrance of Sin. By the late REV. EDMUND CLAY, M.A. Price Twopence.

77, WESTERN ROAD, BRIGHTON.